CROWN CONFESSIONS

Vol.2

L.M. Wyandotte

L.M. Wyandotte
CROWN CONFESSIONS vol. 2

Published by L.M. Wyandotte
Copyright © 2022 by L.M. Wyandotte
First Edition

978-0-578-39071-0

All rights reserved under International and Pan-American Copyright Conventions. Manufactured in the United States.

No part of this publication may be reproduced, stored in or introduced into a retrieval system, or transmitted in any form or by any means (electronic, mechanical, photocopying, recording or otherwise) without the prior written permission of the publisher. This book is sold subject to the condition that it shall not, by way of trade or otherwise, be lent, resold, hired out, or otherwise circulated without the publisher's prior written consent in any form of binding, cover, or condition other than that in which it was published.

L.M. WYANDOTTE

this book is dedicated to the most important people: those who have loved me, those who have hurt me, those who have helped me, and those who have experienced life with me. without all of you, this book would not have been possible. cheers.

also by L.M. Wyandotte:

crown confessions vol. 1
crown confessions vol. 3

instagram: @l.m.wyandotte
twitter: @lmwyandotte

258

the rain on the roof
is like my thoughts
of you. fast and too
much. nowhere to go.

267

this bartender is too talkative.
glass empty. fill it. when it's
got whiskey in it, fuck off.
didn't come here to hear YOUR advice
on my life.
hey! another round!

281

lost track of time. but, never
lost track of the whiskey.

353

waiting an eternity to touch her.
reward could be an eternity though.

420

he doesn't really love you. he's made you comfortable. he doesn't love you like i could. let me try once. clothes on. you'll fall.

459

it's not your ass that turns me
on. it's your brain. know when
one has more power than the other.

479

that day. the one you ripped
my heart out. i'll never forget
it. that was the peak of us. the
old us. no more us. now it's you
and i.

496

instead of us being on top of
our commitment together, you were
on top of someone else.

487

i'd give my last breath
so you could have one more.
only because i wouldn't want
to hear that sound again.

473

i don't waste my time on those
that don't know it could be
spent elsewhere.

394

it's been so long since i've
been in love. but, you remind me
of it. but, love on another
level. soulmate type love.

309

my biggest hope. you felt the same
way. because. then it would no longer
be a question of what if. it would
be when. maybe.

273

i have you at my fingertips.
but, they have never been on you.
so close. yet, so far.

360

i don't want her back.
she shouldn't be surprised.
she fucked up. she knows
she did.

L.M. WYANDOTTE

411

all i want is you. it's as possible
and as impossible as that.

440

he's loved you enough.
i could love you the rest.

463

she called me an idiot.
i never felt so loved.
but, she knows she's a
moron.

481

her in my arms. record spinning.
a kiss from those lips. the little
things in life will keep you
happy. whiskey helps too.

495

tears topped off the whiskey
glass quicker than i could
drink.

322

part of me remains on earth. the
other part left that day.
went somewhere out into space.
fading to black.

284

the sun is coming up. that
means it's time for bed.
one more drink. i'll review
this and the others i wrote
when i wake up.
prolly need a translator.

251

i'll give you whatever you want.
or. at least, all i can give. as
long as i can have you.

354

this heart is for few.
if you get it. don't fuck it up.
there won't be a round 2.

408

my favorite outfit of hers is
her birthday suit. she wears it
so well. amazing. beautiful. sexy.

349

my love for you will outlast
the sun.

393

the day you tell me you love me.
i'll wait as long as i have to.

401

i'm not perfect. neither was she. the relationship was. for as long as it could be. then, i was told a secret. and a fire started. soon there will be only ashes.

438

love is temporary. soulmate type
love is forever. find it.

461

you have my love.
until my breath is taken.
even still. it's yours forever.

466

when you feel the pain the
whiskey pours.

480

looking into her brown eyes
reminds me of real love. the
type i don't need to explain.
because she gets it. she gets me.

492

i inhale whiskey.
i exhale tears.
you get it or you don't.

290

house of 1. 1 plus her spirit.
it's somehow enough for me. to
make it through the night.

358

don't tell me you made a mistake.
you purposely fucked up. more than
once. clearly you didn't learn from
your mistakes. i did though. i
learned to say bye.

418

you ever wanted someone so bad it
consumed your thoughts? then, what
the hell do you know about heartache?

444

you ever been a hopeless romantic?
then what the hell do you know
about love?

470

don't bother bullshitting me.
i already know you're lying.
know how i know? your lips
are moving.

482

if you could see in my mind, you
would know why my heart is black
and cold.

500

your actions echo after
years. hope the moments
were worth it.

366

you fucked up. sorry doesn't fix it. there's no coming back from this. there's no coming back to me. move along. because i moved on.

357

the best thing from us
is something i can't have
anymore. her. and trust.

300

seeing her warms my heart.
because the last one froze it.

259

i can make you think.
i can make you cry.
i can make you laugh.
all without speaking.
just read my words.

330

anything you want to say.
my ears are always open.
just tap on the mic.

367

each time i think of when i lost
you. you slipped away. and i
slipped into hell. on a constant
loop. someone take the needle off.

414

you didn't kill me. i'll be fine.
you killed us. the us that could've
been is dead. rest in peace.

270

i will never get her back.
each day i look forward to
seeing her. at home. but,
she's not there.

252

you're with him.
does he yearn for you like
i do? does he appreciate you?
i would. every hour. every day.
i've written about you. what's he
said?

L.M. WYANDOTTE

457

when you're with him,
do you think of me?
if so. that should be
a sign.

483

i like my women like i like my
whiskey glass, full of the great
stuff and smooth.

497

i'm drowning in a sea of pain.
looking for a safe harbor. i see
those brown eyes showing the way.

314

i forget sometimes i've been through
hell. the devil forgets too. that's
when he realizes i'm not scared of him.
or death. then they second guess trying
to take me.

282

what's next? happiness?
it can get here anytime.
i'll be ready.

344

i wait for the day we can be
together. i don't know the amount
of joy i'll feel. it'll be
insurmountable.

383

you deserve more than what
you get. you also deserve more
than what i can give you.
you deserve so much.

434

i love hearing her sounds.
especially, when i cause them.

484

if you extend a helping hand, it
better have a bottle of whiskey
in it.

499

how often did you lie to me? i
replay words in my head.
they never end.

315

you ever looked death in the eyes?
when he looks back and he blinks,
then you know you're just waiting on
earth til your number is called. if they
call it.

278

she asks about the drinks.
wonders how many i've had. thinks
she wants to join, but isn't sure
she'll catch up. don't worry.
you can have silver.

260

i've yet to touch you.
such a simple wish.
but, the value is in the
wish being granted.

340

give me your soul. i will
be gentle. i will treat it
better than mine. you
deserve that. and more.

388

her smile. little rewards that
remind me i'm not fuckin up.

422

forget about all the bullshit.
it'll pass. if it doesn't.
don't let it win.
fight through it.

460

when you're with me. just don't
fuck other people. is that too
difficult?

475

i don't drink to forget bad
memories. i drink to deal with
them. don't agree? tell me about
your perfect life. not really.

343

just to be with you.
so simple. so complicated.
but, worth the wait.

321

i'll never forget you. you will
always be a part of me. not just
on my body. but, in my spirit.
my soul. forever.

L.M. WYANDOTTE

283

the best plan is to not to
go to bed sober.
otherwise, there'll be fewer
poems.

264

would you wait?
for your soulmate?
how long? eternity?
just got a stack of calendars.

364

i'm thirsty. can i have a case
of you?

439

if we made eye contact, i'm writing
about you in my head. one day
you'll read it.

469

tell me what you want to hear.
maybe i'll say it. if i don't,
i'm sorry. must've been the
whiskey.

493

she didn't lose to another woman. she lost to the woman she could've been. permanent 2nd place.

277

you can ask about the
inspiration for the words.
you may not like it. you may not
get it. that's okay. nobody
gets everything.

338

let me borrow your heart.
i'll pay the debt with
mine. maybe then we'll
be even. then we can share
each other's.

L.M. WYANDOTTE

403

tell me you want me. only me.
that's all you gotta do.
simple.

308

you. i will never forget about
you. forever with me. those eyes.
that smile. that laugh. that face.
the wink. permanent pleasure.

272

he may have you. but, i
have your heart. one day.
i will have both.

253

at night. you fill my head.
during the day you fill
my heart. 24/7.

331

the thought of my hands on your
hands on your body. sexy.

404

not sure if the whiskey helps or hurts
my thoughts. looks like the answer
might be at the bottom of that bottle.
hold on.

454

i found someone new.
you know what she won't do?
forget that i exist.
crazy how easy that is to do.

488

she became my muse for
a while. she'll regret that.

345

every now and then the glass
is empty. find the whiskey.
find it fast. whoa.
that was a close one.

266

my hands on that face.
to hold those cheeks.
rub those lips with my
thumb. to kiss them.
jealous of the one that
gets to. prolly doesn't see
all the beauty.

304

your presence. an unknowing wish
you grant every day. thank you.

374

you're everything i want.
everything i didn't have.
but, i can't have you.
not what i wanted.

427

never touched her. when that day
comes. i'm taking the day off.

468

come back to me.
one more time.
so i can feel you in my
arms. one day.

L.M. WYANDOTTE

494

i was a ship. USS Loyalty.
sunk by your cheating
missiles. congrats. you sunk
my battleship.

287

the plan fell through.
back to the drawing board.
not sure which direction to go.
do compasses help with life?

387

it's simple. i want her. she's
the lottery. for love. for happiness.
peace. joy. i've got the winning ticket.
waiting for the number to be called.

435

i don't know the names of the women
that come by. but, it helps if i
know the day of the week.

471

i am a boat drifting in a sea of time. weathering internal and external storms. looking for the lighthouse of her port. one day i'll find it.

498

i don't need your lips or
love. both have no value. move
on to another investor.

337

i can't touch her. she's right there. so close. heart beating. but, i gotta resist. damn it.

255

there's no such thing as closure.
you never forget. no point in trying.
just think of the happy shit.
otherwise, there's a straight jacket
waiting for you.

407

confession: my love is absolute. you
either have it or you don't. i may
give you a second chance with me, but
not with my love.

456

THOSE eyes.
i don't need to say
anything else. they are
my world.

491

not sure if your past caused
you to fuck up your future.
if so, not sure why i had to
catch the short end of the deal.

313

music sometimes tells me what to
write. sometimes, it's the whiskey.
sometimes, it's both.

257

the bed is empty.
so is my head and
my heart.

362

this whiskey makes me remember
why i forgot you.

421

holding on to my lottery ticket.
waiting for her to call my number.

472

a bottle of whiskey is priceless.
not because of the whiskey. because
of the thoughts and feelings it
causes to come out.

490

there's a dark place in
my head even i'm scared to
go to. there's a sign that reads
"turn back now!". sometimes
i follow the directions.

271

you ever been completely
vulnerable with someone?
heart on the table. naked.
try it sometime. take a
deep breath and live.

256

the sleepless nights.
the whiskey.
the women.
the hole that will never
be filled. but, i wake
up each day with a shovel.
looking for the dirt.

350

tell me your troubles. i'll tell
you mine. we can shake our
heads together.

443

my soul is always singing.
even in my sleep. but, then
it's just a soundtrack for my
dreams.

489

hope revolving thoughts of
your mistakes don't bring
a revolver to your head.

320

out to the stars. where i think you
went. before you came back to me.
i feel you by my side.
thanks for coming back.

268

tell me. how can i be with you?
just be with you. share a meal.
a movie. or even better, a pair
of headphones.

355

someone else has her hand. but,
i have her heart. i have her
soul. 2 out of 3 ain't bad.

441

no matter how much whiskey i
drink. the pain is still there
in the morning.

477

i want your pain. i want your
suffering. i want those so
you don't have to experience
them alone. and then eventually,
they'll be gone.

310

i have love to give you. but, you
can't receive it now. i'll build
a stockpile. so when you can. you can
catch up.

286

how could this happen?
you're supposed to be here.
with me. but, you're not.
some say it's part of the plan.
did they ask you? no. so, fuck their
opinion. and the one who made the
plan.

359

i feel you are not seen as i see
you. not spoken to as i speak to
you. felt for as i feel for you.

409

the whiskey tastes better when
i don't think about the shit
i've been through. also, when
she gives me that wink.

453

don't forget my name.
because you'll always remember
it. and how you'll never say it
before or after i love you.

486

there's no reason to lie.
tell the truth even if it
hurts. that's always better
than fake happiness.

305

a glass of whiskey.
opens the floodgate of my mind.
more words than i can process.
more words than a typewriter
can capture.

261

when i'm gone.
i hope these words are read.
don't take 'em too serious.
but, don't take life too serious
either.

361

don't forget men are people too.
you can't fix everything with
sex. try something new.

L.M. WYANDOTTE

405

do you want to take it back because
the repercussions were not worth
the reward? or for some list of
bullshit reasons?

449

it happened. can't take it
back. just move on.

485

give me that hand.
but, know i'll never
give it back.

451

i'll be nice. but, you
ripped my fuckin heart out.
and. for that reason. my
touch will never be the same.

316

you ever had something you wanted to
touch, but couldn't? kiss? hold?
yeah, me too. she's a masterpiece.

262

it is. a wonderful world.
other words could be used.
but, those are the best and
only ones needed.

437

not sure if it's the ice that
chills the whiskey or if it's
my heart.

326

you don't get to have me. not now.
not ever again. some people
could get pass it. good for them.
go be with them. i deserve better.
sadly, that's not you.

263

my heart is open to some.
it's closed to others.
some have a key.
others have snuck in.

450

you won't forget me.
you won't forget what we did.
you won't forget what you did.
neither will i.

339

to be with her. what is the cost?
i'll pay it. up front.

442

how long would you wait for true
love? how long is too long?
wrong answer.

478

this whiskey helps. helps me
forget stuff i want to. that's
the only trouble with being
sober, the memories come back.

400

don't forget the good times. they'll remind you of ones that could've happened. but. you'll never forget the bad times. the ones that ruined everything. was it worth it?

301

i only have eyes for her.
she knows it. i still like to give
her a reminder every now and then.

265

i was prepared for this.
but, she doesn't know about
my experience.
i'll wait until i can be
with her. it'll be worth
the wait. i know.

415

if i am at a loss for words, it might
not be a good idea to be around me.
unless you got some whiskey. then
maybe we have something to talk about.

455

this whiskey reminds me.
of all the shit you did.
and didn't do. oh well.

279

she's it. she's my person.
my unicorn. only one. only her.

392

you don't deserve me.
you broke my heart and
trust. at the same damn
time. and for those reasons.
i'm out.

413

if you don't make her laugh or smile,
quit wasting her time.

430

sometimes her mouth is open, but her
eyes are shut.
sometimes her mouth is shut, but her
eyes are open.
either way. we're having a good time.

446

oh the nights without you are
torture. but, they're part of
my punishment.

297

if you don't get me.
just keep reading. it'll
click one day.

269

my heart melted when you said
what was in your heart. because
it was the same in mine.
for a moment. we are connected.
maybe again. one day.

431

if i break your heart, it was either
on purpose or it was an accident.
regardless, you're welcome.

458

if you say you love me, i'll
find out if it's bullshit or not.
and if it is. you're blackballed.

288

you know what's worse than being
filled with anger and hate?
no one or nothing to put it all on.
i just cry. then move on.

436

if you haven't gone through any
shit in your life, have you even
really lived?

476

there once was a time you had
my heart and soul. had. no more.
those were withdrawn. deposited
elsewhere.

448

too much whiskey may make me
too honest. may be good for
you. may be bad. oh well. you'll
deal with it.

433

THOSE dark shades cover
THOSE dark eyes. unfortunately.

406

it doesn't bother me to see my ex
with other guys. she was with them
when we were together. why would it
matter now?

432

i tried to give you my best.
instead i received your worst.
not sure who is to blame.

346

i'll give you everything. all of me.
you deserve it. i'm grateful to have
your presence. your majesty.

375

the wait. it's worth it.
believe me. i know because
i know your value. your
worth. and your love
deserves that type of
dedication.

389

clouds covering the sky like i
wish i could do with kisses on
you and rain falling, like my eyes
into your soul wanting to stay
lost for forever.

416

i didn't want more than you could
give. i just wanted you to only
give it to me.

402

don't think i don't know how to have
a great time. whiskey or wine? free
or bound? top or bottom? first things
first. what is your name?

391

the way she makes me feel. not
a feeling i've ever had.
an unbelievable comfort. a weird
funny. a unique similarity. i
want it. for as long as possible.

L.M. WYANDOTTE

377

i want everything for you.
if i can help you get it.
or if i can give it to you.
either way, i am happy because
you are.

347

you ever fell in love with someone
you can't have? then you don't know
shit about heartache.

332

she likes to be with me
when i drink.
she doesn't like to be with me
when i drink.
i like to drink whether she's
there or not.

306

i want to hold her.
but, i fear i won't let go.
not that it would be bad.
i wouldn't agree with those that
want me to. but, i don't care.
only what she and i think
matters. especially. when it comes
to us.

292

you're never alone.
if you think that,
remember your subconscious
will keep you company.

319

the woman. the whiskey. both i need.
both i love. can't live without either.

336

your hand and heart are the prizes
in the race i'm forever running.

365

the music never lies. you just
lie to yourself when you're
listening to it. stop doing that.

384

my heart beats louder for
you. louder when you're
away. even louder when you're
near.

398

if you've ever been burned, it's
not the burn that hurts next time. it's
the thought of, how could this happen
again?

342

i was here when you left.
holding tight. thought that
would be you with me. i still
have so much of you left. with
me. always.

323

i reach my end some days.
by end, i mean end of it all.
but. each morning, i'm back at
the start of the race.

291

only drinking problem i have
is when the bottle is empty.
big problem.

274

my heart is a well of love
and support. come to me when
your bucket is empty.

298

the words for you come
so easy. simple. direct.
full of feeling and emotion.
just like their author.

333

the simplicity of your beauty is
breathtaking. my eyes are
fixated on you when you're near.
i long for when that's all the
time.

378

you don't deserve pain or hurt.
you're too great to receive
those. ever.

397

tell me when was the last time.
last time you wore only pearls?
last time your toes curled?
last time your breath was taken
by force?
can't? maybe we should have a
drink.

275

i had to wait for death.
not like you think. he doesn't
want to come back for me.
he's scared that i'm not
afraid of him.

417

if the glass ain't full, the
piano keys won't move.

372

you prolly won't see these
words. but, they helped me.
they'd prolly hurt you.

317

only pain i feel is longing for
her. every day. the sight of her is a
tease. an optical illusion
of hope and love.

293

it's always been too long
since i've seen you. i
have to see that face everyday.

276

the chats. so simple. so priceless.
only she knows the value.
i can't see a life without her.
it hasn't officially started yet.
but, to me it has. her too.
that's all that matters.

303

a look into your eyes.
allows me a glimpse at your
soul. a soul i want to be a
part of. some day.

334

i dream of falling asleep with
you. i dream of waking up with
you. what happens in between would
be a dream come true.

369

you slipped. and the fall
caused your heart and eyes to
drift. that's why you're
alone.

382

do you know what it means to
wait? really wait? then you
feel my struggle.

325

i don't want you to know what i've
been through. i don't want your pity.
i just want you to not be an asshole.
can you do that?

302

let me hear your breath.
taste those lips.
feel your heartbeat.
then i can see your soul.

289

her remains remain with me.
forever. so does this feeling.
i want her back. i'd take the
exchange. in a heartbeat. so she
could have hers back.

312

talk to me. i wanna hear your hopes
and dreams. hope they involve me.

370

you don't deserve my love. i was
all in. i was there physically.
i left mentally when i knew about
your need to be with someone else.

395

i don't drink to forget bad
memories. i drink so i can
deal with them, without losing
my fucking mind. you got another
way? good for you.

L.M. WYANDOTTE

426

she asks, how long will i wait?
i point to a clock without a big
or a little hand.

474

i've not forgotten how to make love. i just don't remember the feeling of being in love when making love. it'll come back to me. eventually.

399

the sound of her voice.
a soothing, peaceful, happy causing
feeling. i wish i could hear it
all the time.

363
why don't you believe me?
the whiskey wrote this.
not me.

307

sober me and drunk me both
struggle. with neither of us
having you.

294

people wear masks.
but, they don't see
them until it's too late.
some mirrors don't work.

386

you forgot. it was supposed to be
just me. now i am gonna forget it
was ever gonna be just we.

462

who orders a shot anymore?
just leave the bottle when you
pour the first one. thanks.

467

my heart is messy. so, i fill
my chest with whiskey.

385

eventually. you'll realize. you fucked up. but, it'll be too late. so late. i'm already gone. best of luck with the next one.

335

dark colors look great on her.
they compliment her eyes and
hair. like my hand could compliment
her or my lips could compliment
her.

280

few things sadder than an empty
bottle. an empty heart is one
of them.

373

each time i go to sleep.
i hope the dream i have of
waking up to you comes
true. one day.

423

with or without you.
that makes me happy/sad.
you're lucky if i get
that feeling about you.

464

there's always a joke somewhere.
may not be appropriate. doesn't
mean it's not funny.

380

i don't know if it'll ever happen.
i hope it does. that's all i can
do. somehow, something i can't control
would get me closer to her.

329

too bad. she fucked up.
otherwise, we'd still be
together. maybe.

296

if i see you in public
maybe say hi. not just
because. but, because you
care. if you don't, i'll
assume you don't and keep
walking.

368

you said i love you while you were with someone else. you sat in the wrong lap while saying hollow words. now, i gotta right it all. without you.

410

give me your hand. you won't get
it back. but, i'll give you my
heart and soul in trade.
deal?

447

it's bad when the whiskey feels
your burn as you drink it.

465

don't break my heart.
if you do, just forget
my name. or the thought
that i thought you existed.

L.M. WYANDOTTE

452

i forgot how to love you.
wasn't easy. neither is
thinking about why i don't
anymore.

412

my head is filled with thoughts
of her. and song lyrics that remind
me of her.

376

you're priceless. but, you
see your worth limited.
as it has been for a while.
sorry for that.

341

love your sounds. all of them.
the ones you make and the ones
you don't know i hear. 100%
all you and i love all of you.

318

what happened to loyalty? just me.
just you. no one else. why is someone
else needed? if you give me an answer,
that's why you're single.

379

your smile means more than
mine. compromise. it's worth
it. so are you.

L.M. WYANDOTTE

424

if you ain't gonna give 100%,
don't say that four letter word.
either of them.

327

i can't deny how i feel.
been pure since we shared
feelings. forever connection.

285

what's the point?
what do you mean?
isn't it obvious?
if not, keep asking.
that should point you in
the right direction.

348

i'm a loaded gun of emotions.
pointed at her.

381

i want to. she wants to.
but, timing is off. damn timing.

419

woke up. no whiskey. no paper.
no ink. no cigars. i'm going
back to bed. maybe tomorrow
will be better.

351

sometimes, i don't have words. and that scares me. should scare you too. who's gonna tell you how to feel if i can't?

299

up at night. thinking of her.
not enough hours in the night
for me to dream of her.
at least i can do that until
i see her in person.

311

i'll pour my heart out.
i hope you get a cup full.
maybe a refill.

295

tell me your secrets.
i will keep them with
me. they will stay.
even if you don't.

356

my love doesn't stop.
her faithfulness did.
so, i ran out of love.

371

few know. few were involved.
many will be hurt. none more
than one.

324

she knows who she is.
there's no secret.
all i think about. can't help
it. every day. yes, it's a dream.
it'll come true.

328

the rain pours like my tears
for you. never ending.

390

one day when you weren't looking,
i snuck into your heart. i
don't plan on leaving.

352

you think the devil is scared
of you? actually, it's the
other way.

425

stop playing defense against
yourself. it's fuckin up my
plan and yours too, i'm sure.

396

i would've rather her have had
a long life without me. than
for me to have a long life
without her.

429

not sure what women want. if it
has something to do with me, they
got the number or the address.

445

waiting isn't the hardest part.
thoughts during the waiting are
the hardest part.

428
with her pieces and my pieces,
they just fit. perfectly.

L.M. Wyandotte is a prolific poet who writes on the theme of love and loss. He has been writing for many years, and considers his life as still being written.

crown confessions vol. 2 is his second book.

See more of L.M. Wyandotte's work at:

instagram: @l.m.wyandotte
twitter: @lmwyandotte

www.ingramcontent.com/pod-product-compliance
Lightning Source LLC
LaVergne TN
LVHW051400080426
835508LV00022B/2904